1/19 1/0?

With special thanks
To Martin Kerr and Amy Schneider for beautiful book design.
To Helen Exley for believing in my work and your constant wise
counsel throughout this project.
To my husband Jim, for everything.

Published in 2002 by Exley Publications Ltd in Great Britain.
16 Chalk Hill, Watford, Herts WD19 4BG, UK

Published in 2003 by Exley Publications LLC in the USA.
185 Main Street, Spencer, MA 01562, USA

www.helenexleygiftbooks.com

12 11 10 9 8 7 6 5

ISBN 1-86187-421-9

Edited by Helen Exley. Printed in China.

Written and illustrated by Susan Squellati Florence

*Helen Exley Giftbooks cover the most powerful of all human
relationships: love between couples, the bonds within families and
between friends. No expense is spared in making sure that each book
is as thoughtful and meaningful a gift as it is possible to create: good
to give, good to receive. You have the result in your hands. If you
have loved it — tell others! We'd rather put the money into more good
books than spend it on advertising. There is no power on earth like
the word-of-mouth recommendation of friends.*

When You Lose Someone You Love

a journey through the heart of grief

WRITTEN AND ILLUSTRATED BY

Susan Squellati Florence

A HELEN EXLEY GIFTBOOK

When someone we love dies, a part of our own self dies too. There are no words deep enough to describe this time of sadness. I had a dream after my father died, that I was shot in the dark by a stranger. I lay on the ground, on my stomach, not knowing what had happened. I didn't know if I would live or die. This dream is exactly how I felt after my father died. We are physically hurt when someone we love dies. We don't know how we can go on.

It takes time and a thousand tears to accept the death of someone you love. Stay with this sadness. Your tears are holy water from the deep place of your loving.

You will receive great comfort from people who have been in the place of sadness, where you are now. They will be friends, family and even people you have not known before. In our sorrow, we are all connected.

I hope this book will comfort you in your journey through the heart of grief. I hope this book will bring you peace in understanding that there is something that lives forever. This is love.

*When someone you love dies,
a part of yourself dies too.*

For as much as the one you loved
did not belong to you,

your heart belonged to them.

You were a part of each other.

There is a physical hurt
within you.

It is as real
as the emptiness that surrounds you.

You will wonder
how you will walk
in a world
that no longer holds
the footprints
of your loved one.

You will wonder
how the world
can go on
when your world
has stopped.

You will speak silently
in the language of tears,
as your heart seeks to understand
what it cannot.

Spiritual thoughts,
religious beliefs,
and philosophy
may not take away the hurt.

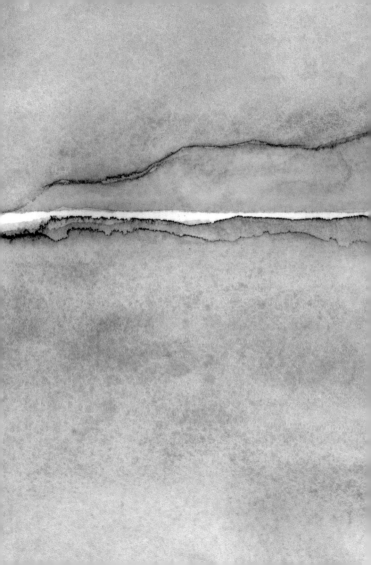

But the power of love
will comfort you.

love will comfort you

Love will be found
in the hearts of those
who surround you
and care about you.

People who have been
in the place of sadness
where you are now,
will be there for you.

The sun will continue to rise.
And the moon and the stars
will still light the heavens.

*You will begin
the sacred daily ritual
of "remembering."*

Your grief will become
your companion...
The part of you
that is compassionate,
and strong, and deep.

In your suffering
you will be given
  the greatest challenges
you will ever have...

To be able to accept
what life gives,
and what life takes away.

And to be able to accept

the mysteries that are a part of life.

Peace will come to your days.

Peace

will come

Peace may come
with the early morning sunlight
streaming in your window

Or peace may come
with the song of one bird

With time
the veil of sorrow
will lift.

Peace will come to your heart

and you will know
    this love we share
    is an eternal gift.

You will see
what is most precious
and most sacred
is the love we share.

This love lives forever.

ABOUT THE AUTHOR

Susan Squellati Florence

The well loved and collected greeting cards of Susan Florence
have sold hundreds of millions of copies in the last
three decades. Her giftbooks have sold over one and a half
million copies.

   With words of gentle wisdom and original paintings, Susan
Florence brings her unique style to all her gift products and
her readers have written time and again to thank her and tell
her how the books were a profound help to them. People have
told Susan that her words speak to them of what they cannot
say... but what they feel.

   Susan Florence's completely new collection of giftbooks in
The Journeys Series invites the readers to pause and look
deeply into their lives. "We all need more time to rediscover
and reflect on what is meaningful and important in our own

lives... and what brings us joy and beauty. Writing these books in The Journeys Series has helped me understand more fully the value of love and acceptance in helping us through the difficult times as we journey through life."

Susan lives with her husband, Jim, in Ojai, California. They have two grown children, Brent and Emily.

THE JOURNEYS SERIES

1-86187-420-0
Change... *is a place where new journeys begin*

1-86187-422-7
How wonderful it is... **Having Friends in Our Lives**

1-86187-418-9
On the Gift of A Mother's Love
For my mother from your daughter a mother too

1-86187-419-7
Take Time Alone *The gift of being with yourself*

1-86187-421-9
When You Lose Someone You Love
...a journey through the heart of grief

1-86187-417-0
Your Journey
...a passage through a difficult time